T0106101

STAINED WITH LIGHT

T. Obatala

iUniverse, Inc.
New York   Bloomington

Stained With Light

iUniverse books may be ordered through booksellers or by contacting:

iUniverse
1663 Liberty Drive
Bloomington, IN 47403
www.iuniverse.com
1-800-Authors (1-800-288-4677)

ISBN: 978-1-4502-0250-3 (pbk)
ISBN: 978-1-4502-0251-0 (ebk)

Printed in the United States of America

iUniverse rev. date: 8/9/2010

Stained With Light

Through the whites
of your eyes,
past the wildness,
down to the white
meat of your skull,
white finds you curled
at day's end.
white finds you
stained with light.

Tongues

Golden is he
who comforts the dying,
the speaking of tongues
tamed by love, the skin,
folded lips, the hardened aureole,
the reddening of the cheeks.
Askant the truth. Less of self
is what is deeply feared.
Don't hate the Devil.
He has spoken stupidly for years.
Mortal man, woman is dumb.
They don't need the high road.
When they look back silence
kills the silence.

The Long Sad Faces

I hate them for their
ingratitude.
I am tempted to throw
things at them.
They are forcing me
to go agape.
They don't care about
the things we care about.
We are slowly disappearing
as they are always there.
How silly we must seem
as they always make us
accept the walled-out,
weighty things.
We go missing.
Often.
They wait in the grass at dawn
as all the paraphernalia of our
pass comforts are stamped out.
They want to come in.
You were not, you explain,
ready for guest.

Some, Most

Some die
in a silence
that rises up
from the toes.
Some try
to breathe
out light.
Most hate
what they
have become.
Some see
dying as
a manic
self love,
forever pledging
the impossible,
Promising forever.

All or Nothing

All the nothing
that this is,
this good nothing
isn't any less than
it was yesterday
or the day before.
The soul parts from
the body because
it must. These things
happen. Nothing, Soul,
Suffering, they abandon
us and try to find their own
way home. They must.

Suddenly This Defeat

You know you know
your life is over
Know this is hard
on you.
Suddenly this defeat
You thought you had
more time to warm the body
But the body just takes to
the cold hills
To face as much harshness
you could bring it
The body is more
than the body
It can manage
in public
Even now the landscape
is losing itself.

Following The Wrong Gods Home

The air thins
Faith asks for more
Faith rocks back and forth
in rage and grief
Everybody's working seventy
and eighty hour weeks
Everyone's lost faith
Everyone hates faith
Even the little ounce left
in anyone's heart

The Waiting

The exceptional crime
was that mother was
a remorseful drinker
of whiskey and cornbread
and father was the weeper.
Here comes the moment
you've been waiting for…
Hope can be a given
glimpse of a better way
of being.
And so I am thinking
of forgiving you, father
mother.
When it hurts, it hurts.

The Good Man

Muscle shakes its fist.
Soul leaves the body.
Heart has an altercation.
Cold comes from every corner.
The woman cannot find her brother.
Leave it to me to believe that I am
a good man.
The first man to
speak a silent tongue.

This

Who would choose
This for himself?
This is worse
Than the unmerciful
Hours of your despair.
You must approach
This with an air
Of cautious pleasure.
This…
We spend years
Describing This,
Avoiding This.
You don't have to be
Good.
This is a struggle.
Did you change your
Life?

You

We live
In a world
Of distance
And motion
Where the mind
Is dead
Where the body
Is a cadence
Of blazing evening
Light where you wake
Up from a restless
Night of dreams of you.
Only of you.

Keeping Time

The naked taste
Of boredom proves
That he is sleepless
Because his eyes are
open.
Never to be here/anywhere.
Nothing but empty graves now.
A skein of bones keeps time.

The Bottom of It

I like that it is Spring.
That you are here.
That we talk about
folks who don't have us,
badly.
We're asking questions.
We'd like to know more.
We're getting to the bottom
of it.
People let things drag until love
dies.
Not us.
We have it.
When the lights come on
we can see better.

Kahlil

We metabolize loss
as fast as we have to.
Something in you remembers
that pain loves pain
but it is far too late
to re-invent your life.
I am 39 years old
watching my youngest
brother lose his battle
to scag, watching him
pick through his few,
meager belongings
to give me something,
though in my memory
we're neither here nor
missing
but sleeping.
No, not really sleep
but through for the night.

What The Dead Have Forgotten

I've become
a stunt double
for them.
It's as if
between
the invisible
timbre of
their
dreams,
for a brief,
startling
instant,
like a slight,
small spasm
in the back,
I have been
blessed with
their longing.
I'm filled
with
what
the
dead
has
forgotten.

Delicate

Just enough to cause
A slight stirring in the throat,
Somewhere beneath the words
That betray those little acts of will
That never seem to matter most of the time.
We always want the ones that will slay
Anything for us. Not just the dragon.
The ones that can make the suffering
we don't always see become bone in spine.
So subtle, like infant sleep
You know I want you helpless.
It is how delicate we are later we might be wiser.

Somewhere

There is fog
Somewhere
Near someone's
Window.
Someone moans,
Somewhere near
The end of town.
And so, someone
Could be anyone,
Anywhere.
Alone and huddled
Where the world
Is white and they
Are barely alive
But still believes
There must be
Something very
Beautiful in the body.
The secret of this
Journey is to not
Lose sleep over
Anyone, at any time.
And maybe pray for another
Birth.

Not As Brother

Not night
always meeting
Itself, not night
as brother or
bully,
this is night
that has had
it.
No book of the night.
No rules of courtesy.
Light is only a vessel.
Night is made
for
blood
and
bone
only.
I cannot stop
myself from thinking
of you.
There never is
a place to end.
And never was.

Doing Their Job

This heavy industry
of others,
just being alive
for and with
each other
has nothing
to do with
happiness.

I empty myself
of the names
of all the others
that are happy
and reach for
a shotgun.
It is late
and the hours
have done
their job.

The Places of Themselves

If surrounded by the right
things life is fun when you're
good at something good as this
stupid Brady Bunch sentiment hits
you square between the plexus. Here
comes the evilness, the jostling between
the good that begins low in the soul
it is simply the weight of the dark itself
that slides off like mist when dawn finally
arrives you stand aside and pray
and watch them everyone
becoming the place of themselves

Zero-Point-Zero

Today the earth is dry
and resounds like a drum.
Again, today, night will fall
in no time.
Imagine or remember how
the road at last led us to
a world that appears now
at zero-point-one-zero degrees,
the only one that bursts out
of the silence.
World of a thousand eyes viewing
a thousand things at once and each
thing no more equal than the next.
Don't let the world that is blocked
by my shoulder disturb you
any longer.
Your country is with me.

The Brutes

Are rough.
Have a weak shape.
Black.
Like an entrance
to their anus.
Greet each other.
Go up in the dark.
Lose themselves
in silky and black
currents.
No easy deaths.
Best friends were
missing and loneliness.
Chaplin warned us.

The Other Side

This is the place
Where I will die.
It is as eerie as
a dream. When
I come back it will
be go time once
again but be aware
that the mind
stays dead forever.
This is not
accidental.
You will never
come to being
yourself ever
again and the wind
on the other side is wild.

Crocus

Night falls
for everyone
and harder for some.

What he almost was
looking forward to was
the brilliant agreeableness
of air that was proclaiming
another new day that once
again began his small murders.

He knew she had him when he
told her he could not live without
her scent, crushed purple blooms,
creamy lotions, crocus and cedar wood
rubbed in almond oil.

And all this before noon.

What if someone brushed
past her and then looked back?
It was enough to drive a man crazy.
He was going crazy.

Cesare Pavese(1908-1950)

Doubled over, I hide in the shadows
of the farm in Calabria. The moon rises,
casting a little shadow also, in the vineyard,
along the ravines, and over the women, beautiful,
with jars on their heads. My love is one of them.
I only offer you dumb words, questions like do you
love me, will you be my wife. On mountains and valley,
bright sun shines in like hard labor. I have spent so much
time fighting the Fascists, my eye of blood, for you, my
dear, is always pointing the other way.

Out Of Thin Air

Maybe the mind
works like the broad
promise of a beginning
that wants to stretch its
fine lines to infinity then
vanish. Of course, one
way to believe this is to
pretty much take pleasure
in knowing there is no point
in having a mind if hatred only
finds its way to construe
conclusions out of thin air…

The Angel

The Angel appeared
where the smell of old
grass kicked through
just past and near where
the church took the "hell"
out. The-Son-of-God-Holy Spirit
part was next to go but the Angel's
face, it *had* a face, was a separate
thing from the sky and he saw that
the planet was part of our loneliness,
that the planet needed to be rescued
from the same un-nameable thing,
that was cousins to the loneliness.
But as all angels are wont to do,
She just stood to the side and grew
smaller and smaller.

Trakel (1887-1914)

Bewildered by their dreams,
deadly weapons embrace the dying
warriors when all roads end in black decay.
I am forced to greet the heroes, the bloodied,
defeated of Galica as night leans down with a
thorny wildness. This day I lose everything
because of you, my fair Wittgenstein. Enough
of this explicit chemistry. Why am I so afraid?
Red clouds gather silently over the meadow. I will
leap happily into the grave to join you my brothers.
The silent world is more palpable than your prayers

Vladimir Mayakovsky (1893-1930)
Love letter to Marina

My love,
You have done more
than inquire about me. My verses has reached you
and for that you were persecuted. You must have gone
to bed one day and come to terms about your terrible fate.
No matter that you have a full family, husband, daughter, son,
I am only a latrine cleaner who doesn't give spit about marble.
I have no cause to wake or trouble you. By your love of me,
    you
must be my wife of Socialism. With respect, you have taken
    my
buried verse that seeks to balance natural sorrows, pains,
and hurts. And I would only rather compose romances for
    you.

Come in

If you think about death enough
it sort of belongs, makes sense
and then it will keep on meaning
nothing. The wasted lives continuing
with a stunning persistence until the darkness
of their hours takes them. It is time to die.
Come in.

Marina Tsvetayeva (1892-1941)

Because of her admiration for the poetry of Vladimir
Mayakovsky, she was considered Pro-Soviet and was
evacuated from Moscow. Having had her husband murdered
and daughter twice imprisoned and herself unable to write or
published, she committed suicide.

What has angered you so my God?
And why must so many be killed?
Let's just say the incident is closed.
Give me back my husband, my country, my voice.
I'll return to the place of battle and hold my
grief close to my breast. Blood, only blood you
give me and poems are useless. You can tell this
at a glance. In the madhouse of the inhuman, I
refuse to live. I know you most Godhead! I am sick
to my marrow bone. I have no more need of my chimney
city Akhmatova. I see nothing but black billows of smoke
in your grace God. Look deep to find any grains of hope in
this life my brothers and sisters. We will wait together,
in exile, in the next

Forgive Me

What I believe in
changes nothing
in this world.
Not the intelligence
of my hands nor even
your very own martyred voices.
It is as if we are standing past
the lilting cries of the newly dead,

Company

The light in this room
covers everything.
Enough problems, enough
things to fill a book.
The early morning with
sun wrapping itself
meditatively around parts
of the little kitchen
table leaves me with hours
and hours of my own dumb
company. If I live forever,
I still would never believe
that the underside of light
is light. I want to be left alone...

Dark Light

It could have
been the accumulation
of years on years
of failure but why
do I pick this moment
to remember this?
I have not flourished
all of last year
and this one
promises no solace
also.
Only
dark
light.
dark,
dark
light…

Their Places

Look,
the dead hold
their mouths
like this, no,
more like in their
hands as if trying
to catch the cries
of the good and vanished.
Themselves.
Themselves like someone
who has no belongings.
Like those who are tied up
and left to the hands of those
who destroy everything they touch.
They are dead and when we try
to listen they always have someone
taking their places.

Aleksander Wat (1900-1967)

If there is no bottom to evil
then there is no end to irony.
Poland, Russia, Lubyank, all Siamese
sisters of death for me. With the "Great Purges"
everything now is different. They do not understand
the curse of the poor. Don't burn my magazines. Nothing
is more real than boredom. I want to drink and sing songs.
Not this cursed work, work, work! They wake me every night.
I can't get their skulls out of my head. My lips grow dumb.
Bah! Work!

I Turn For Home

In this thin
And birdless air,
In the full light
The only things that
Matter are wordless.
Each day this is what
I am waken to, "When
Will the wind no longer
Carry my mother's voice.?"
Is it today?
Will she die today?
Will her last words find
A way to reach me before
The ending of this false dawn?
Here in February, the name,
The weight of this horrible,
Horrible disease falls on this house
And every house like this one and yet
The eye of her memory comforts my
Own miserable little life… enough.
I turn for home.

Tadeusz Borowski (1922-1951)

Together, Dachau, Auschwitz,
stands looking into the distance.
Once these were my two countries.
One the gas chamber and the Auschwitz
flame, the other a rotting grace in the Smolensck
forest. But that is enough. I became famous by choosing
as my death the fate I escaped when the odor of the distant
meadows was my blood when I was arrested. Dachau, your
inventions were perfect. Your brother, Auschwitz, invented
murder for me. I gas myself as if the world exists only through
us and nothing has changed.

Squeal

I know there are small saints inside of me.
It is a lovely labor to be accepted by anything
Or anyone but these days faith in anything good
Is rare. The closest things we find in nature to divinity
And God is light and soon that won't be much support.
That is why I have lined all the angels in a single file
By height and weight to be shot. Their voices are little
'oh's and 'ooh's and 'ah's. They have become certain
The small sacrifices shown to me were good portions
To save some of them. Most are terribly still and say
Nothing. They do not believe in playing with the facts
Of their inevitable demises and know to complain,
To squeal, would be pointless.

Symphony of One

I have become
a perfect symphony
of one as the hour
sweeps into the next.
Under my skin, blood
has been replaced
with light. My body
has become a willing
prisoner of itself.
When I part the air
nothing stirs.
No thing.
I have no reason
for moving.

My Body Becomes a Flame

Before the
resurrection
of apathy
has begun
to set in,
in the scented
air, in the full
face of the moon,
I find myself
belonging to no
one; and so, that
is no moon that
I am looking at,
and this is no
place from which
no one returns.
My body becomes
a flame.

Good Molecules

What I can tell you
is that it is awfully
quiet now. With
every heave
you disappear.
The cold vapor
from your
nostrils quickly..
then slowly
fills this tiny room,
all good, good
molecules,
suspended,
a
shrill
cry
until they
have
illuminated
this
page
for
you.

The Wind Still Pounds

For some unbelievable
part of a moment you see
your friend Lydia walking
past her leaves in the Jewish
part of her town, see her trees,
feel her change and it is some
kind of a beautiful, relaxed thing.
Suddenly you are thirteen and with
every freshly picked leaf comes fear.
The wind will soon try to pry away
every part of this slumlord owned,
poor, rickety, overcrowded, tenement
foundation. Ten people in two rooms
stuffing newspapers, plastics, cotton,
hair and rags into windows and floorboards.
You knew what you had to do. Keep
stuffing, keep stuffing, keep stuffing.
And you crammed the sweet, black,
honey of summer into those dry walls.
For hours you will try to sleep but cannot.
Soon it will be winter and you will be cold
for the rest of your life.

RipRap

You see
them for
some
unbelievable
part of a moment
just before they
leave this riprap
piece of life,
your dead ones.
'You don't need
luck' you coo to
them in soft, slow
voices.
Just come back.

Shuffle

He was a man
comfortable with his
own color but beneath
the great weight of all that,
things were beginning to get
out of hand. Maybe he was a little
too comfortable. He takes short walks
to avoid their anger. He knows with this
calm many violences will come to him.
He, more than any other creature on this
planet must learn the trade of silence, to
build houses of light,
to shuffle…

The Back Of Beyond

I live in the back
of beyond.
It is a cemetery
for the dead and poor
where they attend classes
that teach them that nothing
now can ever come to any good.
Another professor sternly admonishes
us for not doing more with our lives.
He has been dead for a long time.
Someone in the other life stapled one
of his hands to his forehead for refusing
to salute the King. Just looking at him
leaves a chill in the body if we had one.
The new recruits are led away to their little
deaths and are told not to think of any misery
for there is nothing that is not here, there or is.

To Nandia Anjuman

Was the dinner ruined
because you were writing
poetry? No, poems shouldn't
smell of you. It was probably
a busy time that evening
as you bantered and bargained
and begged for more time between
the oppression, death and light.
You must smell more of cheese,
curds, yesterday's eggs; more
of the things that matter to your
family, not of something so beautiful,
as your words.

Matter

Some called
and said that
they were shocked.
I told them it's the way
each moment looks to
the next one.
It's been this
way pretty much
since you died.
You left before
I had time to comfort
you this
exclusion
of other
sensual
matter...

You Don't Know Me

A piece
of sky,
winter
light is
in love
with the
pure
geometry
of itself
as my own
blood traces
the length of
the horizon
and the stars
are fools who
know nothing
about me.
Nothing.

The Beautiful Trouble

The heavy Sun
believing that there
really is safety in numbers,
called on his best friends,
Moon and Wind, begging them
to say goodbye to this, the old life,
and leave the humans to their own devices.
Suddenly there were flocks and flocks
of pigeons sweeping just over the horizon
like a bitter silence that came to burden us.
Ignore the last poem I wrote you, my dear.
I believe your cheating ways brought on
the whole goodbye of this earth.
All our beautiful troubles are because of you.

Keep Me

This is how you are
Supposed to pray.
Let me not grow
Crazy for things, for power.
Does the bear thinks
He invented himself?
I don't know how to pray
Easily, which in
A way is a prayer.
If I had another life
Will the story about Jesus
Still be a good one?
Will the earth remember me?
Where is the man who killed my brother?
Those who know run out to silence me.

Forgive Me

What I believe in
changes nothing
in this world.
Not the intelligence
of my hands nor even
your very own martyred voices.
It is as if we are standing past
the lilting cries of the newly dead,
on the lawn of a beach, waiting
for the moment
when anything,
or anyone
forgives
us.

Good Life

My life walks
all night through
numb and solitary
streets looking for
its own life. The simple
truth is I wish that one
of them would make up their
mind and get over themselves.
My real life is as startling as the
inmost secret of a good, good life.
I want him back.

My Only Swerving

The bones
of my body
if broken
a certain way
can generate
light on their
own.

That is why
I can say
the thing
that I was
the thing
that now
waits,
has turned
into a funeral
lamp.

I think hard
for all of me.
Light jumps in
where my body's
been.

Nothing to Recant

That's just
it. I have
nothing to
recant. Finally
my eyes have
darkened with
kindness and oddly,
even for anyone,
everyone. When
I move, the air in
front of me becomes
the only thing not happy
to see me. Some fear
I might not show up at all.